FIRST EDITION

Library of Congress Cataloging-in-Publication Data

Christensen, Elisa Dawn Fortise

**ISBN:** 9798697570845

To Merlene &
Terry —

With Much Love —

Lisa Christensen

## Other Books by Elisa Fortise Christensen

The Fentanyl Warrior: How I Got Off And Stayed Off Opiates

Raising Boys To Be Honorable Men

The Finest Thread: A Love Story

The Teen Warrior: Raising Addiction-Resistant Kids

The Far Away

Available at:

**https://authorelisa.com**

# All of This

## Poetry for Real

Words by Elisa Fortise Christensen
Art by Megan Monroe

To see some of these poems performed, go to
**WWW.AUTHORELISA.COM**

Allow website to fully load, make sure your sound is on, then scan the QR codes in the book next to selected poems with the camera on your phone.

# Table of Contents

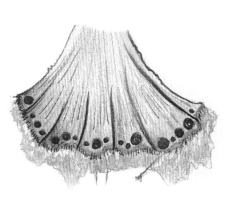

All of this...

Existence

## Giants

In my world of golden light beams,
Firing synapses and electrical impulses,
The thrill of touching my lover's skin,
Or the narcissistic, heady scent of jasmine,
I fancy myself a giant.

We all seem so,
riding this wave
of mortality,
Concerned over
lasting impressions,
Securing a foothold,
While delaying the inevitable,

As if....
We have some semblance of effect.

Yet we know the secret,
The story of what exists,
Although its magnitude goes far beyond,
Our minuscule perimeter of understanding.

The truth, while all at once completely humbling,
Provides me a gift beyond all the finest of fortunes.

I am so barely conscious, vaguely aware,
Of this 80 or so years-a lifetime,
That appears to be so solid,
As it speeds by like a bullet train on nitro.
A lifetime-a year-an hour-a minute-
And I am gone.

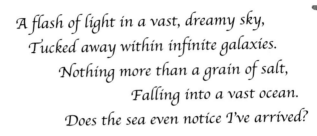

A flash of light in a vast, dreamy sky,
Tucked away within infinite galaxies.
Nothing more than a grain of salt,
Falling into a vast ocean.
Does the sea even notice I've arrived?

In the mirror I study my shell.
I see the roadmap of my emotions and experiences,
All of the laughter, the countless tears,
The hurt under which I have crumbled,
The ecstasy of certain moments that have lifted me from this
rock.

I gently stroke my lover's skin,
Silky and creamy,
Its softness glides under my fingertips,
And I remember—
Every climax, every smile that formed for only me,
The sound of his breathing,
The impossibly heady, dizzy drift of love.

My child lays his warm, golden-white head,
Gently on my heart as he listens to my body,
Which hosted and delivered him,
And forever longs to protect and encourage him.

Every last molecule within me,
Rises gallantly to celebrate this love.

A question remains.
How do I reconcile,
The insignificance
of my existence,
With my human ego,
that leaves me
Always struggling to declare
my importance,
When in fact my time here
holds no weight at all?

My footprint on this plain
is that of a flea,
Surrounded by
stampeding elephants at best.

My remedy, then, can only be-
Perhaps an idea good enough to gain a foothold,
Or maybe my legacy, as my sons pass on my faint
footprint.

4

As I inhale,
for a moment
I pause,
For I realize,
however fleeting,
That this singular
breath is really,
My biggest miracle of all.

For even as I am
less than
a flash of light,
Next to the blazing sun,
As we all are,
I am a miracle.
A true giant.

# Moccasins and Boots

Have my hiking boots
Fallen on this earth,
So ancient,
Where your moccasins
once found their way?

Have my companions' paws
stepped amongst the prints
of your wolves?

Am I walking amongst
the gentle giants
That once sheltered you
from fierce gales?

Did you wonder about me as I now do
about you?

Does the young hawk that glides above us come from
the blood of the ancient one who also soared your sky?

In centuries past, did you stand
amongst these giants and think of me?

In my quietest moments.
I can hear your laughter
deep within this forest.
I can smell your hearth.
I can see your camp,
and taste your buffalo.

I can feel your hope,
Your delight in this beauty,
I can taste your tears
over the ones you've lost,
Feel the joy over the new tickle
deep within your belly.

I know you.
Just as the woman
on this mountain,
Hundreds of years
from now,
Will be here.
Quiet.
Wondering...
If I was thinking.
of her,
As she is now
thinking of me.

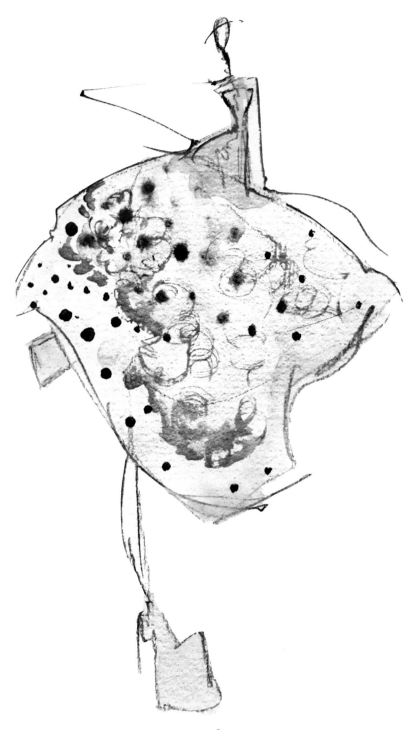

9

# Second Chances

If you were offered,
A real second chance,
Would you sign on,
For a backward glance?

To correct your errors,
Clean up the mistakes,
To avoid the costly pitfalls,
Every one of us makes?

Would you go back for that kiss,
That you were too shy to get,
Or say yes this time around,
To that skinny dip at sunset?

Would you listen to our little ones,
Laugh more than you did?

Would you make love to your lover and,
Not always be right instead?

What if it's true,
That when we die in the end,
We see our whole lives,
Played over again?

Who would you ask to leave,
Who would you let stay,
What would you want
in your movie?
What would you throw away?

If life had a do-over button,
Which moments would you choose,
To play over and over again,
The ones you never want to lose...

Is there a person you didn't love,
Quite enough for your heart's fill?
Is there a dance with someone,
You have yet to finish still?

I would start over as a child,
So I could parent my baby me,
I would give her so much love,
She would be my number one-She,

I would give her the parenting,
That she needed to grow with ease,
The security and comfort,
That would never, ever cease.

But wait! If I start over,
If I go back, erase any part,
I'd be changing what shaped me,
The scenes that have molded my heart!

There are no second chances,
Do-overs don't exist,
There's no auditions,
Not even a waiting list!

Life is pedal to metal,
From the womb to the soil,
And it is up to us,
Whether we soar or whether we toil!

My life has been hard,
Full of pain and tragedy.
But taking second chances,
Is just not for me.

We are all a brilliance of colors,
A kaleidoscope colored sea.
From all of our joys,
As well as our tragedies.

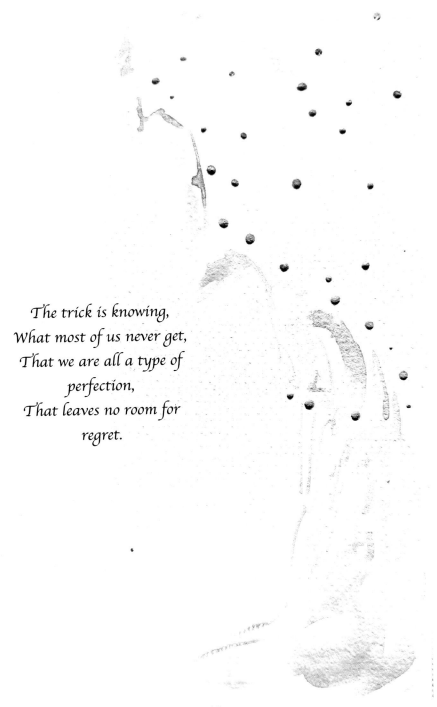

The trick is knowing,
What most of us never get,
That we are all a type of
perfection,
That leaves no room for
regret.

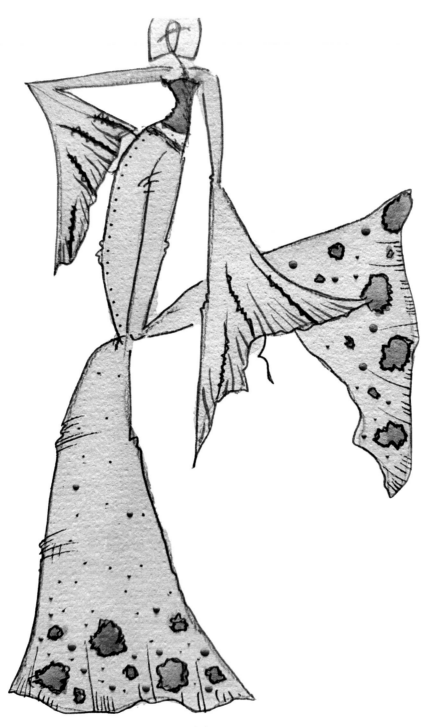

14

# Searching In Tongues

If yours is Allah
And mine is God,
We can't both be right,
So it's gotta be me!

Don't agree?

Then let's battle,
Bloody and long,
For the ultimate right.
To name that song.

You are a sinner, a blasphemer,
Clearly a freak!
If my god is not THE god,
That you seek!

I am correct,
You are just plain mistaken.
All but _my_ god,
Must be forsaken!

Haven't you read the script?
The papyrus and holy grail?

YOU, my friend, are clearly,
Going straight to Hell!

What?
You say the exact same thing
to me?
Your god is the god?
That's an impossibility!

I'm afraid I must kill you now,
Wait, while I give this trigger a squeeze,
Or maybe by a bomb,
With relative ease.

God is in all of us, you fools!!
She is everywhere!
The trees, the ocean, the earth,
She is the air.

Or maybe there's no god at all,
And this is all that there is.
A bunch of idiots causing pain,
High off of religious bliss.

Either way, I know this,
I have found god for
certain,
God's not in the Sky,
Or behind a magic curtain.

God <u>is</u> us, and <u>we</u> are <u>she</u>,
So simple,
So pure,
So just let it be!

A microsecond in the entire scheme,
Don't waste it squandering!
Choose love as your wing,
And tolerance as your theme.

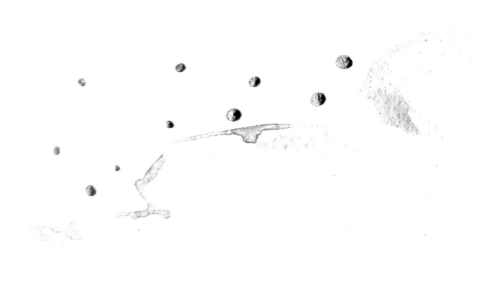

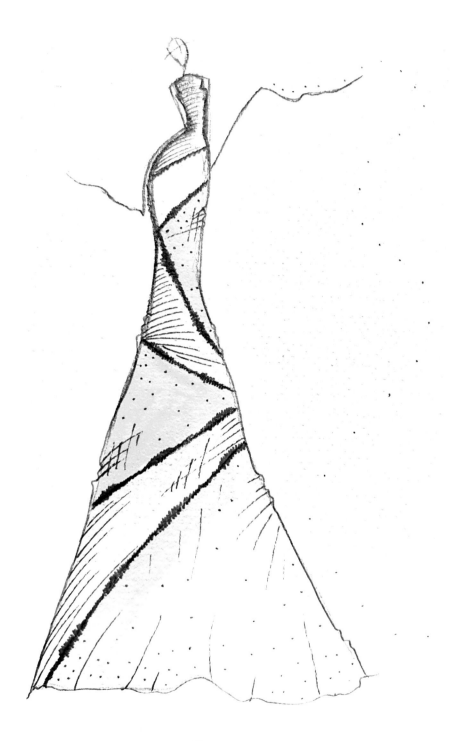

18

# Opting Out

So at 47 I have arrived.
A position most disconcerting,
Troubling? Nay,
Downright disturbing!
A blatant assault.
An ego in default.
Should have steered left,
Perhaps joined a cult.

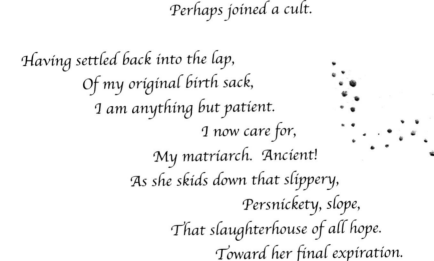

Having settled back into the lap,
Of my original birth sack,
I am anything but patient.
I now care for,
My matriarch. Ancient!
As she skids down that slippery,
Persnickety, slope,
That slaughterhouse of all hope.
Toward her final expiration.

Once a beauty of,
The extraordinary kind.
With the quickest of mind,
Don't get it twisted.
Aging is nothing if not unkind,
Names of her clan,
She now labors over to find.

Her once glowing blonde tresses,
Sexy, 50's signature dresses,
Athletic leaps,
Impressive all night sexual feats,
Replaced now with falls and wrinkles.
A faint frame, once sturdy,
Now wobbles and crinkles.

I shall have her feet, it appears,
Worn down from all those steps,
As I look at her and upsize,
The navy blue faded from her eyes,
Now light gray, I see my own,
Reflecting this unsavory demise.

I say...

"Nay!!!"
Launching a rather
Loud and inappropriate protest.
With all of my feisty lather,
I attempt a half-assed jest!
But I'm not joking.
I am not.
Gravity.
What a horribly, shitty guest!

I opt out!!  I simply do.
This aging process,
Perhaps it's for you,
But certainly not me.

"This is a far cry from a thrill!"
I protest with an icy chill.
(Excuse me for just a moment,
I must go take another pill.)
Sore joints, crows feet,
Vision going South?
I have had my fill!

You must understand my decision,
Appreciate my unprecedented position.
I'd happily pay for the botulism syringe,
Carefully dodge sunbeams that offend,
From beneath my wide brimmed hat.
I order my fine potions.

Please!
Ship STAT!

Getting any older?
Nope.  Not doing that!
I opt out!

Yes, you heard me,
I simply won't go.

I've called the 1-800 number,
About losing my glow.
What about my sexual, slippery slide,
Threatening a possible dry run?
Not happening!

My feisty partner laughs and says,
"Princess Vanity,"
you have no choice here!"
I say "Nay!" "I refuse!"
I'll even give up my lavish festivities,
The entire month I decided to show,
If I can get this aging thing to slow!

You enjoy getting older,
But I'm showing aging the door.
I shall remain the way I am at present,
Don't care what's inevitable,
It matters not who says it.
This girl is aging no more.

I opt out!

All of this...

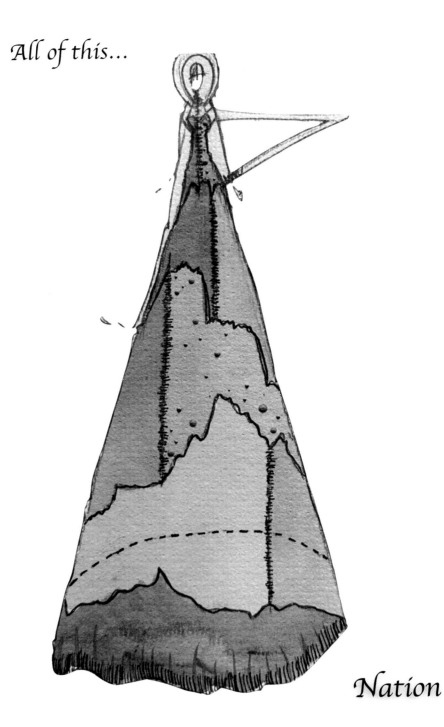

Nation

# America

You used to be the epitome,
Of true promise from your very birth,
A home bursting with inspiration,
One of the finest places on Earth.

You shined with possibility,
Fairness for all. Equality.
You glistened with so many dreams,
Sewn together with golden seams.

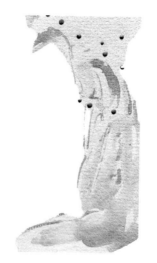

We flocked to you, the outcast,
The downtrodden, exiled and poor,
We poured onto your soil,
Delighted with all you stood for.

A new start seeped in fairness,
We all hoped for that one chance,
We loved you for your freedom,
You showed us hope at a glance.

What happened, my dear country?
Was it the true state of your start?
That we brutally slaughtered your natives?
Violently ripping out your heart?

Then went on to bring pure evil,
Onto your golden shores,
As sick as our previous slaughter,
We brought you slavery's bloody horrors.

And one hundred and more years,
Have slipped by in a blink,
What have we accomplished?
I shudder at what you'd think.

Now the strongest world power,
We flex for all to see,
Yet our children, so many starve,
Millions suffering in poverty.

While our kings of Wall Street rule,

Live fat upon the land,
How far have we really escaped?
From England's royal sand?

We tout you as Home of the Brave,
We brag about our land of the free,
Must the things that we desire,
Come with such a fee?

We torture, maim and kill,
We bully and invade,
While ignoring the very principles,
On which this dream was made.

We shun equality,
Like a pauper in the street,
We take your sacred flag,
And stomp it under our feet.

I want to again stand proud,
I want our pursuits to actually have meaning,
I want to us to help our downtrodden,
Our stars and stripes brightly gleaming.

I want to have the freedom,
To practice what was promised us all,
Freedom of religion without issue,
Our very roots, don't we recall?

Yet our corporations now rule,
Like tyrants on the throne,
And suddenly we somehow all feel,
Segregated, so very much alone.

I want us to reunite,
Remember why we're here,
Overcome our hypocrisy,
And press through all of our fears.

I want to feel enamored again,
With this majestic place of my creation,
Standing proud on the highest hill,
Proclaiming "This IS the greatest nation!"

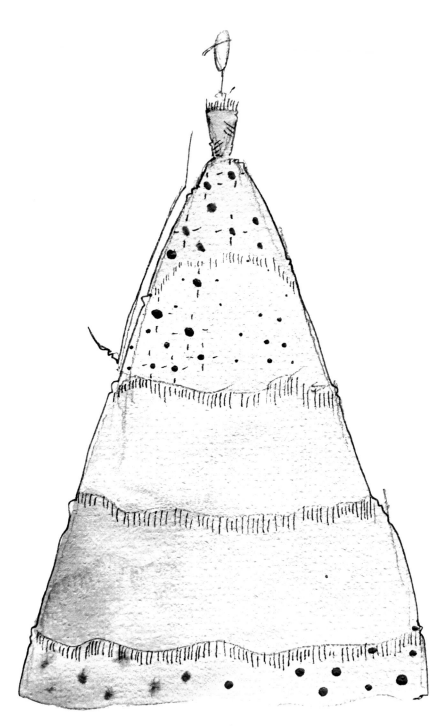

## I Don't Want Your Politics

I don't want your politics.
I don't care about your red or blue.
I'm just tired of my planet suffering,
For the benefit of a few.

I don't like your policies.
Or your interest in my womb.
I just know what I know.
Without change, it will all end soon.

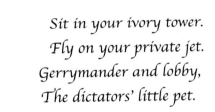

Sit in your ivory tower.
Fly on your private jet.
Gerrymander and lobby,
The dictators' little pet.

What's happened to this great land?
Freedom is slipping away.
The news is labeled fake,
Human rights lie on the fray.

Temperatures a-rising,
Ice is melting fast,
Species disappearing,
Our world is not going to last.

I don't care about your politics.
I want a safe place for our kids.
Where there are no guns in schools,
And freedom is not a bid.

I want clean water and food,
I want our veterans, old and ill,
To get the care they deserve,
I want this mess repealed.

I'm scared and I'm sad.
I'm heartbroken and under attack.
I don't care about your politics.
I want our future back.

## For You, I Cry

Were you washing dishes when the knock came? Or maybe you were in his room, lovingly folding his civilian clothes for the day he would return.

Were you smelling her pillow and smiling as you remembered how much your little girl loved strawberry shampoo?

What dreams did you discuss with him for when he returned? A marriage to his high school sweetheart? A home purchase just down the street?

Can you still see her riding her pink bike with the tassels on the handlebars and worry about her falling again and scraping her knee?

They will always be your babies, Mama. Even when that knock came to your door. Even when your heart fell through the floor. Even when you took your last breath from your old life and became a ghost. Even as that soldier told you your baby gave the ultimate sacrifice.

Even when they offloaded the casket. Even when they handed you the neatly folded flag. Even after everyone left and the crushing silence of your home without them there swallowed you whole.

They were your baby first, America's soldier second.

32

All of this...

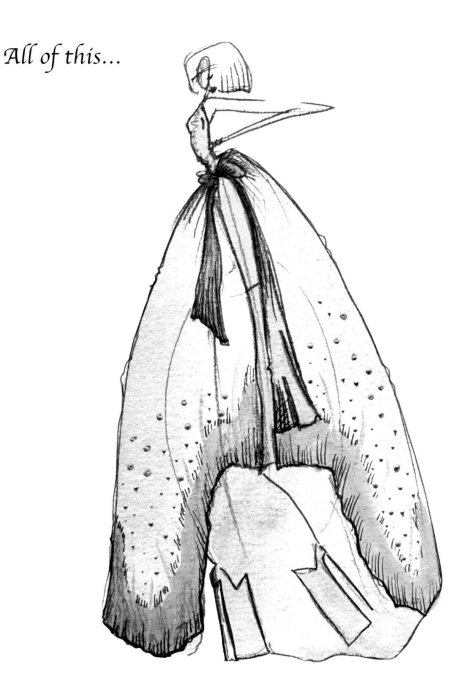

Addiction

## Our Greatest Affliction

Addictions, restrictions, convictions, decisions,
A needle, a bottle, step down hard on that throttle!
Disaster. No more laughter. Destruction for years after.
Placate, eradicate, fornicate, masturbate.
Addiction. Restriction. Addiction.

No more art, no more heart,
Another false start.
No more honoring love,
Through God's sacred benediction.
Just destruction, restriction.
Addiction.

Give it a go!  Run that prop right over top of her, Skipper!
Hell yes!  Sounds like fun!
Ours souls through a wood chipper.
Addiction: a rather benign sounding word, don't ya think?
Let's call it what it is: Jack The Life Ripper!

Slots!  Cha-ching!  Sex!  Food!  Anything!
Addiction?  No way!  I just like to play.
Hypocrisy, a democracy run on big Pharma.
Don't think about it...sure!  It's all real!
Here's your script for a thousand more pills!

Addiction. Prison. The System. What a waste!
What a horrific affliction in this human race!
Disgrace. Sadness.  Do overs don't exist.
Annihilation, frustration, desperation!
Another slit wrist.


Artistic brilliance being pickled
nightly in a skull.
No more compassion,
no more money, no more love.
Losing it all.
No more light in your eyes dear,
Now they are black and so dull.


Addiction. Why?


Is getting through a human life
really that tough?
That we all have to medicate,
With this poisonous stuff?


Addiction.


Don't say you don't know,
you hypocrite you,
We've all been there at some point,
to something, it's true.


35

Don't give me your shit!
Don't tell me you're fine.
Doesn't matter who's is worse,
yours or mine.

Addiction.

I'm SICK of crazy land!
I want off of this ride!
No you cannot have me,
Mr. Jekyll and Hyde!
I'm so angry I had to say goodbye
to such a noble king,
Way too early because of this
Jack The Life Ripper thing!

Addiction.

As a mother I'm simply scared out of my mind!
How do we get our babies
through a world so unkind?
How do we keep them from running
straight into it blind?
They won't listen. Most of us never do.
Premonition! Please! Not them!
Not addiction!

For three years I watched in agony
my greatest love dissolve,
Destroyed, I moved on, tried to get back my resolve.
From the frying pan straight into the fire.
This is not my sanctuary,
this is another addict's funeral pyre.

Addiction.

The human condition
comes with such a design flaw.
We should come with two bodies,
not just one!
The first to ride hard and wild,
toss it out when we're done.
Then step effortlessly into the second,
shiny, new and clean,
And live the rest of it out,
perfectly pristine.

Unfortunately we don't, we get only this one.
And when we go hard for a little too long,
The damage is done.

There's no going back, no saying,
"Oops! My bad!"

Because now you are screwed,
nothing more scary or sad.

Addiction.

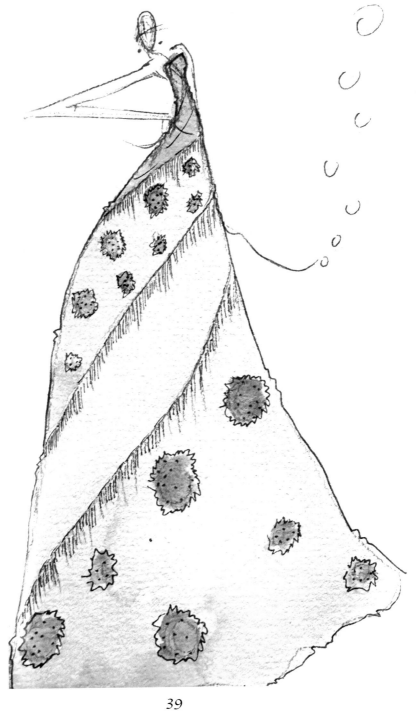

# Befriending The Dragon
## (For Levi)

Far-reaching beast, poised to kill,
Approaching, king of all fires,
Instinct, you offer him the fuel,
What you desire, what he requires.

Snarling, hissing, he shoots at you,
His elixir, so fiery and corrupt,
You shiver, convulse, draw closer,
Awaiting the moment he will erupt.

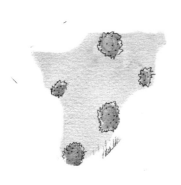

Smoke, burning deeply down your throat,
Huge claws rip and shred your skin,
A sacrifice, a generational curse,
And you are his villain all over again.

A shoot out is your newest request,
So romantic, but don't you see?
Whatever it is you ask for,
Is exactly what is going to be.

Somewhere deep in the dank den,
Of your dragon, unrelenting and fierce,
Is a shaking, terrified, little boy,
The one we've all loved over the years.

But the dragon gets ahold of your core,
Ripping and clawing at your soul,
You just don't seem to understand,
The high price of a dragon's toll.

You pay with your life, my sweet one,
And those of your little babes,
Whatsoever it is your dragon offers,
He will steal all of your days.

I realize his path is easiest for you,
Since you've grown so familiar with him,
I understand the only home you've known,
Has been his filthy den.

But my brother, please be aware,
This time the price is too high,
If you remain curled up with your dragon,
You can kiss your whole life goodbye.

Please, my sweet, blood child,
Stop for just one small moment and see,
With your finest courage and endurance,
How beautiful your life could be!

I do promise you there exists a world,
Outside of that old, familiar den,
Only here will you ever find peace,
And discover where your life can begin.

But no one can do this for you, brother,
It's your soul path, your battle alone,
Scoop up your innocent, little babes,
And with all your strength, finally come home.

## We Wish We Could Rescue You
### (For Teddy)

We wish we only knew you on your good days.
Not the days your speech is slurred,
Your eyes are dull,
And you struggle to walk.

We wish you weren't killing yourself.
We wish those of us who love you didn't have to watch.

We wish you weren't so entrenched in your addiction.
We wish we could rescue you.
But we can't.

That's the thing about addiction.
It's a lonely game.

The deeper you go, the less we can reach you.
Someday, probably much sooner than we realize,
We will bury you.
It will be a truly heartbreaking day.
The lost potential.
The lost friend.

Another lost life.

Do you realize just how deeply you're loved, Sweet Teddy?
We will fight for you, but it won't do much good,
Unless you are willing to fight too.
We don't want you to take your last breath,
Way too soon.

Just know, Sweet Teddy,
We all love you so much.
But us saving you isn't an option.
That is up to you.
But if you will fight for your life, so will we.
So will we, Teddy, so will we.

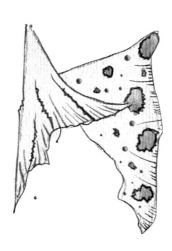

All of this...

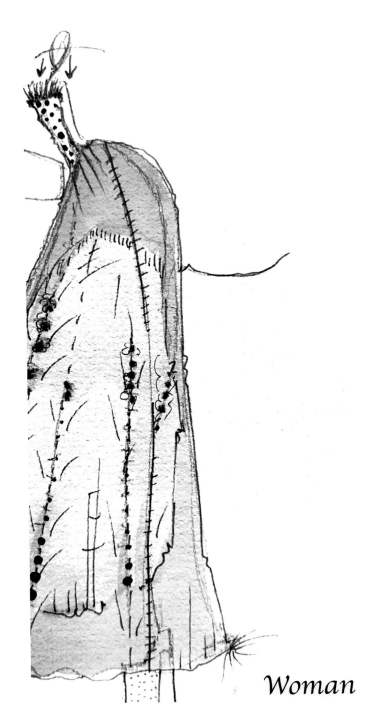

Woman

# Chiseled

A woman is not chiseled,
Out of the books she's read,
Or the greatest knowledge
in her head,
Or even the mighty kings
that she's bedded,

Instead...

It is her path.
A deep haunting, a soul-longing.
A painful compilation of all she's befallen.
A wrenching of her very existence.

Her rebirth.

What are we but a flash of light,
In a Universe of many.
A flicker of a flame,
That burns out before it almost begins.

How small our lives are,
Yet we consider it all worthwhile.
Our babes are our immortality.
Through them we live.

48

But what of us as a whole?
Who then are we?
Our tender lives, so fragile, like a firefly.
So brief, they rapidly rush us by.

I want to live knowing there's more,
something grand.
I want to construct this life from my gut,
And every day take a stand.
For all of us, for this land.

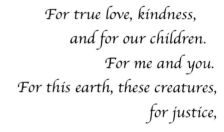

For true love, kindness,
and for our children.
For me and you.
For this earth, these creatures,
for justice,

For what's true.

What has happened to the heroes
and heroines in our world?
Not the ones you see in the same, old films,

But the ones that demand
mercy, kindness,
Justice, peace?

Our heroes.

I'm a heroine and I'm chiseled as such,
And I vow to chisel my sons as much,
Rear them to be true men and kings,
We need more true kings.

Join me, if you have the courage,
And wake up from your stupor,
I implore you!
Be kind, courageous,
Gentle to one another,

And our Earth.

Be Good.
And maybe, someday,
We can save ourselves,
From ourselves,
After all.

51

# A Dog That Sleeps On My Head

I'm ok alone,
I'm ok just being me,
Because I've made it,
Through the stormiest of seas.

I'm too old to be cool,
Still young enough to be hot,
But firm in my denial,
Of what I am and am not.

I can talk intellectually,
With the greatest of ease,
But I've almost forgotten,
About the birds and the bees.

Shocked by my crow's feet,
I've learned not to smile,
While looking in the mirror,
Cuz it cramps my style!

I'm bitter, you know,
Don't believe anymore,
Think no one can be trusted,
So let me show you the door.

I apologize for offending,
It's not my intent,
I'm sorry you feel your time,
Wasn't well spent.


Just look at it this way,
You wouldn't have liked my bed,
It's full of sadness,
And a dog that sleeps on my head.


Keep your chin up, don't worry,
I'm just damaged goods,
How to heal?  Believe me,
I wish I understood.


But I'm okay though
Rearing my little men,
Okay with the thought,
That I'll never love again.


I'm great company,
And there's always my books,
Just living life alone,
Avoiding the hooks.

Don't know what happened,
Where it went off track,
But I'm pretty sure,
That I'll never get it back.

I'll always have my intellect,
And my beautiful boys,
What do I need you for,
With all of your noise?

I wish you the best,
In all that you do,
But leave me be,
Because I'm scared of you.

I'm ok alone,
I'm ok just being me,
Because I've survived,
The stormiest of seas.

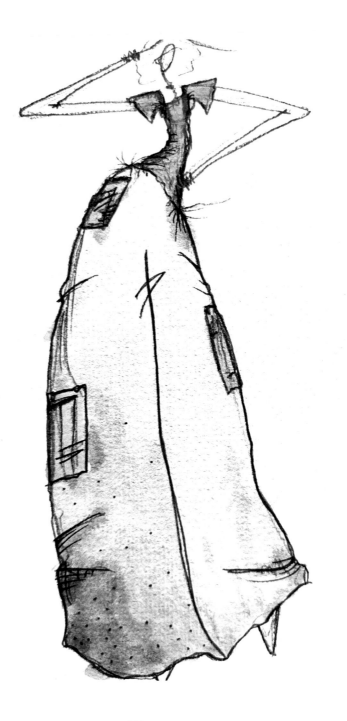

# Skidding In

Give me crazy,
Give me wild,
Not interested in tame.
Miss me with mild.

I want to bite,
Not just lick,
I want pure passion
And make it quick!

If it's high, I'll jump off it.
If it's deep, I'll swim through it.
If it's tough, I'll surely do it.

Choose easy?
I think not,
Give me a challenge,
And see what I've got!

And if I have to,
I'll do it alone,
I go big,
Or I go home.

It ain't easy,
Don't I know.
Living life fast,
And never slow.

Breaking all of the rules,
Coloring outside the lines,
Living pedal to metal,
Then paying the fines.

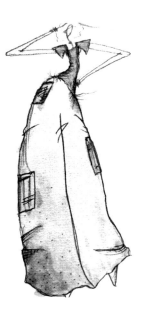

It's true big thrills,
Don't come cheap.
When I lose,
It cuts me deep.

But when I win,
I win it all!
So well worth,
Risking that fall.

Don't bore me with average,
I won't sit still,
Don't even approach,
Unless you're all thrill.

                              Give me messy,
                        Wild and fast,
                  Even though I know,
                  It may not last.


          Sweeping vistas,
          Brilliant greens,
          Deep blue oceans,
          Red hot dreams.


    And when it's all over,
       I'll come skidding in,
          Knowing for sure,
          I'd do it all again.

59

# Petrichor

I collect you like tiny drops of dew
on a caladium leaf.
A broad net thrown deep into
the ocean of my experiences.
You are my gold pieces I keep in my pocket,
To jangle around when I need soothing.

Diamonds of light
dancing on a desert lake.
The honeyed warmth
of my newborn king's crown.
The earthy crunch of giant's
jewels under my boots.
The lullaby whispers of aspens.

The spray of sandy sea froth
on sun kissed skin.
The languid silence
of snowy mornings,
The succulence of a lover's kiss.
All collected and accounted for
In my sacred vault.

I treasure you like rubies
in a smooth, cedar box.

The buzz of tiny
hummer wings.
The electric blue
of big mountain sky.
The round delight
of my pregnant womb.

And the seductive scent of forest rain.

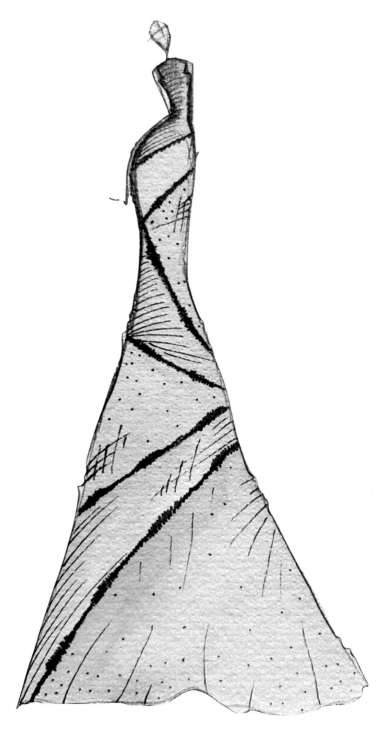

# Fear

I whisper so quietly
all of my fears,
Thinking they're not real
if no one hears.
I wedge them in silently between
the waves of my dreams,
Amidst all of my laughter
and blood curdling screams.

I fear a lot of things
that shouldn't be told,
Like the fear of aging,
or worse: <u>not</u> growing old.
Even more than that,
I fear for my sons,
Fears so damned scary,
they leave me stunned.

Deep in the night,
equally deep in my bed,
These fears refuse to whisper,
they stomp through my head.
Like disrespectful children
with clogs on their feet,

They hammer away at me
with every heart-beat.

I should know by now
that things do mostly work out,
But oh my fears!
Can they ever shout!

I've decisions to make
bearing impact and force,
Decisions that could change
my entire life's course.

Mostly, though,
I'm afraid of me,
Of all that I am
and all I should be,

And if it's the truth
I must confess,
I fear my failure, yes,
but even more, my success.

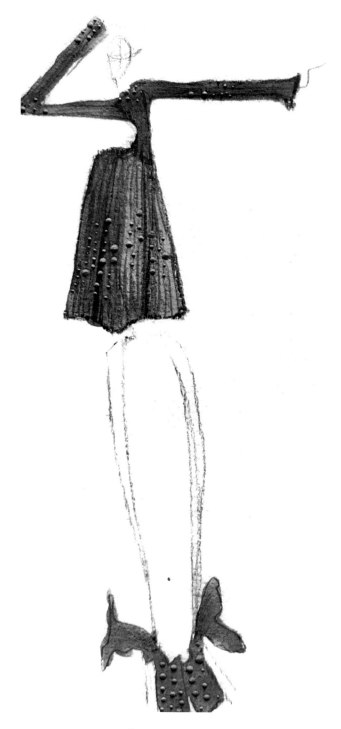

# Evolving

At thirty I rode the wind,
Galloping around in my flawless frame,
Wearing my war paint,
Concerned over how I landed in your eyes.

My shoes hurt,
My ego bruised easily.
I lived for your admiration.

I feared the loss of my "wowness,"
My power to command a room,
Just by floating through the door.
I measured myself by your response.

Fifty is different.
It took adjusting not to be able to
take your breath away with my curvatures.
I had to face the truth.

Oh but the treasures I have gained!
I didn't just muscle through dark nights,
They turned into long, haunting years,

Where my soul
wracked me in pain
as it expanded.

My face now boasts all of those moments,
In smile and frown lines that are here to stay.
My body, with all of its scars and challenges,
Still gets me out of bed each day,

And for that I am grateful.

Now I have something different to offer.
All of the battles
with their losses and victories,
Have carved me into a soul first,
A body second.

I bring you wisdom,
Insight,
Compassion,
Patience.

I offer you truth,
Depth,
Peace in my soul,
And love.

*Love for myself,*
*Love for you and your imperfections.*

*The lens of life is different now.*
*More significant,*
*More meaningful.*
*And so it is.*

*Aging.*
*An unexpected gift,*
*A master of mystery.*
*A curator of character.*

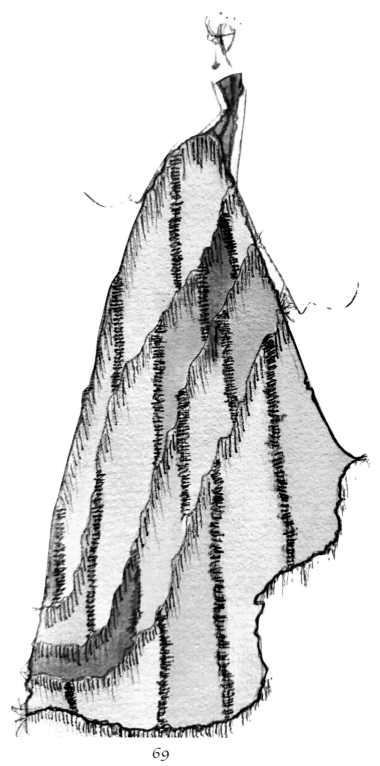

# Good Company

I know it's confusing you that I'm not returning your calls.
After all, who am I to abstain?
As an uncoupled, 50-something female floating freely along this plain?
Do I not realize? Am I dumb or slow?
Do I need society to put a price tag on my worth once again?
After all,
I'm considered not whole, don't you know?

But here's the thing, and forgive me if I offend.
I've built this woman up from a smoldering pile of destruction,
Brick by brick by brick.
Because I survived and grabbed that second chance,
I'm a wee bit picky now on who I pick.

You see, I no longer need you.
And wanting you, well, it's a matter of taste.
There's no need for me to make haste,
Good women don't expire like old milk,
We are composed of the finest and strongest thread, like silk.

It took me decades to get here.
Fighting, clawing my way out of the darkness,
Learning to sit quietly and for the first time know myself.
I'm not cocky, just discerning.

No more broken glass, no more static, no more loud horn honking.
Just music.
That's all I need.
Sweet, delicate music.

So please stop honking your horn at me.
I'm not blind. I can see.
And I'm not scared to just be with only me.
After all, it turns out.
I'm pretty good company.

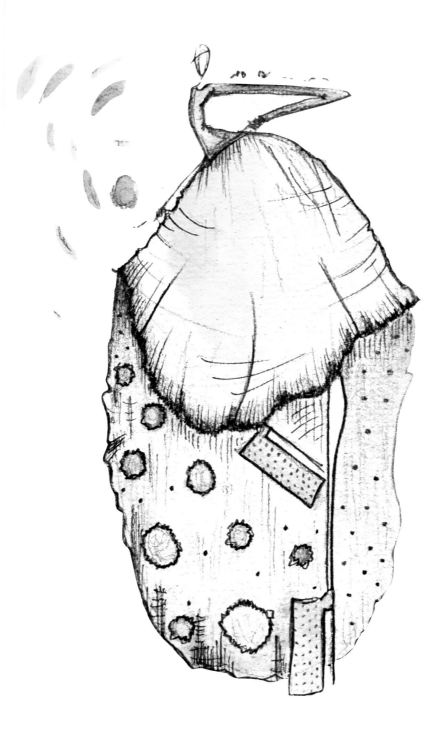

# I Dare You

What do you fear, dear soul?
That has not been faced before,
Throughout thousands of generations,
Within ancient civilizations?

I dare you, brave girl,
To stand like the warrior that you are,
On that cliff edge,
Bellowing out your war song.

I see you, fearing your power,
But why?
Why did you listen to them
Who dared tell you you weren't enough?

I dare you to take back your power,
Not tomorrow, not when it's convenient,
Not next week, when it won't impose,
Right fucking now!

Take it back boisterously!
Make a hot mess of it,
Make a nuisance of yourself,
For all who try to stop you.

73

*For my girl...*

*You are imperial,*
   *Resplendent,*
*And most definitely superlative.*

   *Who are you to dim your light,*
      *To fill the world's fat yawn?*
        *Bullshit!*
     *Don't you dare hold back!*

   *For you are everything this world needs:*
        *Courage,*
        *Tenacity,*
        *Fortitude.*

   *Grab your gloves and go!*

All of this...

Love

## Welcoming You

You really want to know who I am?
Are you interested at all,
In what lies behind the pretty face?

Perhaps in search of,
A little substance?
A certain grace?

Not unlike any other Mother
Of this great Earth,
I am strong.

I've had to sharpen my skills,
Thicken my blood to ward off
The night's chills.

When the dragon came,
It was solely my game.
No knight,
Not even any armor,
In sight.

So I fought.

Bloody, impossible battles.
That wore me down
to the very bone.

Alone.

But not to worry,
For you see,
That is what has
made me,
Well....
Me.

Still residing in that lofty tower,
Delicate whispers disguising
My hard earned power.
No true knight in site.
That's strangely been...
Alright.

But even within my intricate castle,
That I built up around me...
That shell.
That forms my layer of protection from,
Those crafty, hungry beasts from hell,
Who come cloaked in,
The black of winter's darkest night.

I am still just,
A vulnerable girl.
Bathed in golden light.

I have read all of the words of the great men,
And when they no longer took me to,
Those beloved, mysterious corners,
I began to write my own.

When the colors of my paints,
Finally blended into a dull hue,
So faint,
I created new colors.

When my feminine frame failed me,
In the physics required to cross that wide moat,
I designed the proper tool.
I learned.
I built a boat.

Should you find the courage to approach,
The strength and tenacity necessary to hack away at,
The wild, glorious, flowering vines growing without reason,
Surrounding my castle,
Season after long season,
And you are afforded,
A fleeting peek at the treasure within--
I welcome you.

Let's begin.

Should you get past those tall, outer gates,
That were built by men of much lessor character.
Those who dared to show,
With absolutely no honor or truth,
Somehow slipping past my barrier.

Those who dared to win the girl with fancy spins,
Across the parlor's gold and pearl inlayed floor,

Please stop there.

Pause just a moment at that door.
Before approaching again.
Stop and take it all in.
Really see what your greatest journey
Has brought you to.

Open your heart and really look.
Realize what all of this took.
For this is the destiny,
Of your soul's greatest dream,
And yes, I am even more real,
Than I seem.

The laughter you hear
but cannot quite determine,
The direction from which it comes.
That is indeed pure joy.

The tears that fill your eyes,
Are those of knowing,
A sweetness rarely found.

It is truth, not magic.
However tragic.

That thrust of purpose you feel at your back,
That skip suddenly quickening your feet,
As we approach to meet,
That is all real.

No magic spells have been cast.
There's no fleeting, shallow, trending romance here,
That couldn't possibly last.
That's the next castle over.

What is here is real.

It is a lifetime of commitment.
An incomparable dedication to truth,
Decorated equally with my hard-earned scars,

As much as my finest beauty and the ecstasy I bring,
Along with more thrills,
Than a man has ever seen.

You are not in a dream.
But you have discovered,
The hidden treasure that is me.
So welcome.
Approach with care.
I'm so glad to finally see you there!

At my castle's great gate,
Finally realizing our extraordinary destiny,
Our sweet fate.

Welcome.
I've been expecting you.

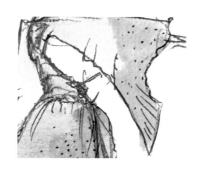

# Thrilled

My love, have you finally found?
That my steps don't even touch the ground?
My head's always wrapped in a fog,
And I'm caught singing to the dog?
It's all because you thrill me.

I chase you around with a crazy hunger,
And feel decades younger,
I sleep smiling big, ear to ear,
My stories are all bouncing with cheer,
Yes, my dear, you thrill me.

You always seem to have on hand,
A seamless, perfect, fail proof plan,
To launch me past the fat, full moon,
While keeping us in perfect tune,
With just one look, you thrill me.

Just when I regroup my head,
You throw me onto our bed,
Each move you make so spot on right,
I'm higher than the highest kite,
I'm thrilled, simply thrilled.

I try, oh God, you know I do,
To realize that you're mortal too,
But there is simply no disguise,
When you seduce me with those sexy eyes,
You are not from this earth,
Not you.


What is this magic that you wield?
No need for any sword or shield,
With your lightning moves I come undone,
You've got me completely good and spun,
Just flat thrilled.


Yeah thrilled.


It's not just that muscled bod,
It's not your attitude, your cocky nod,
It's you knowing you've got me wrapped,
I'm helpless,
My powers completely zapped,
But mostly I'm just flat out thrilled.

Not just your jitterbug that's got me spun,
It's the intelligent challenge,
All the fun,
Of tangling with my male counterpart,
Being wrapped up in your loving heart,
That always seems to thrill me.

What must it be like to really know,
That someone you love adores you so?
That just your energy in my space,
Is enough to light up my whole face?
No other word will do:
I'm thrilled with you.

Your essence is such pure, straight dope,
You charge me up, you give me hope,
Each day I wake up wrapped in you,
Is enough to ensure I'll soar on through,
Because my love,
I'm thrilled with you.

Someday when you snarly expire,
And there comes an end to all your ftre,
My world will stop spinning and stand still,
And I'll scream out for my ultimate thrill,
For no one does it for me like you.

On your headstone it will say,
For all to read as plain as day,
The message that for sure must be,
Written down for all to see, simply,
"He thrilled me."

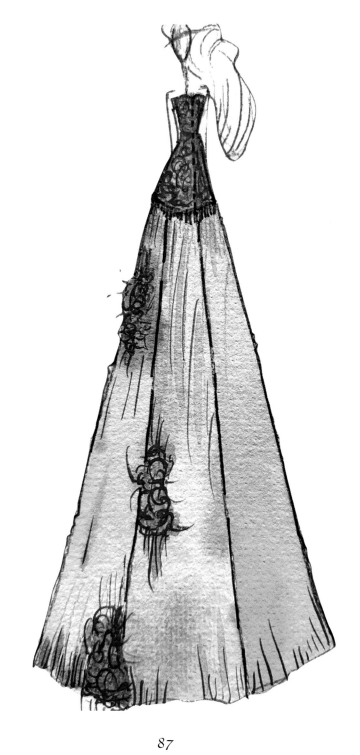

# Grow Old With Me

My dear,
There's nowhere I'd rather be,
Than by your side,
As you grow old with me.

I know we fight and carry on,
We wield our swords for all to see,
But darling I do love you so,
Settle in and please grow old with me.

When twilight sets
and our bones creak,
When sunset
is at the top of our hill,
When our passionate longing
turns to comfort,
It is you I'll long for still.

When our luscious hair no longer grows,
When wrinkles show the many laughs,
When sighs replace sprints and jumps.
You'll still be my better half.

When our children are grown and living large,
When our teeth aren't as white or strong,
For every step I take down that path,
My love I want you along.

When flying dishes are replaced with shrugs,
When our joints groan instead of snap to,
When our lives are like the setting sun,
I only want to be with you.

You are the green in my garden,
You are the red in my art,
You are the harmony in my song,
You are the love in my heart.

I know we sometimes brawl and spur,
I know we talk of ending it all,
But the truth is, there's no one else,
But with you whom I'll take the fall.

You are my strength, my grace, my inspiration,
You are my reflection when I'm at my best,
There's no one like you in this whole wide world,
I choose you above all the rest.

You fascinate me and leave me in wonder,
You spark my passion and calm my bones,
When your strong arms are wrapped around me,

I can exhale. I'm finally home.

Let's walk this plain hand in hand,
But not too fast, let's take it slow,
Come grow old with me, my sweet love,
And we will walk together into the glow.

All of this...

Broken Love

## Shards Of Glass

You arrive in me like sunshine in the air,
A fresh breeze through a dark basement,
Wrapped in warm comfort, joy,
I embrace you for all that you are.

But then you bring out the broken glass,
The million shards of pain from your past.

I see that you are bleeding,
I feel the pain.
I am now bleeding too.

I cry out to you, begging you,

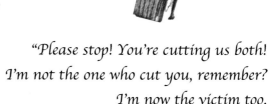

"Please stop! You're cutting us both!
I'm not the one who cut you, remember?
I'm now the victim too.

Please remember, but not too deep,
They are gone.
I'm the one who is here.
I don't come with shards of glass,
I don't even come with knives,
Not one blade.

Just all my love to soak up your blood,
To stop the pain
and finally heal your wounds.

Recognize the white flag
I hold high out in front of me.
Hoping just to know you.
To love you.
To lounge in bliss within
your warm, sweet chamber,
Your sanctuary,

And finally get the chance
to meet the real you.

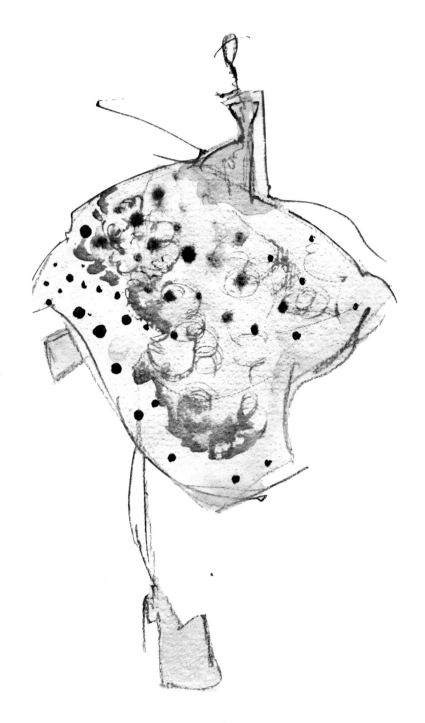

## Shattered

I'll always be grateful and truly flattered,
For tasting the angels' elixir, unsurpassed,
I loved you so much it hardly mattered,
Before we laid our love to waste,
bruised and battered.

I loved you so much it hardly mattered,
Blinded by your million, shiny shards of glass,
Before we laid our love to waste,
bruised and battered.

I failed, refused to see the tattered.
Splinters of your future, forged from
your broken past,
I loved you so much it hardly mattered.

Our dreams of sustaining this ecstasy scattered,
Our time together spins to conclusion too fast,
As we lay our love to waste, bruised and battered.

My god! You were brilliant tho, smooth and lacquered,
So extraordinary, a demigod unabashed,
I loved you so much it
hardly mattered.

# Silence

Silence.
It never could recapture
Our heady drift that existed
Before night was gone.


Such ancient longings.
Sifting through centuries,
Countless lifetimes,
To tap your well spring.


But I did not sign up for your noise.
The words you have chosen,
Wedged between God and mankind,
Have gouged me to my bone marrow.


Yet here I am once again.
Alone.  Splattered.
Against the backdrop
Of love's bravest dream.


I'd have learned, one would think,
That sharp shards of shattered glass
cut deep.
Though clearly,
Not deep enough.

Or I wouldn't be here once more,
Now would I?
Sniffing around
for your sunshine scent,
Longing for something
I never really had.

Languishing in my isolation,
Longing for your embrace,
Picturing your face,
Needing to escape this place.

Nothing learned.
Yet all lost.
Within this
Brutal silence.

# The Kiss And The Fist

Remember when it all started?
Your sweet lips on mine?
Your strong arms around me?
Our lovemaking so fine?

Remember when it all started?
That moment when I first saw,
The monster that you could become?
The night you bruised my jaw?

Remember in the beginning?
How you swore you'd be my dear?
To protect me from any danger?
Release me from my fear?

Remember the first time you shoved me?
So hard my head hit the floor?
Or the time you slammed my face?
Into the back of our bedroom door?

How am I supposed to reconcile,
Your kisses along with your fists?
How can my knight in shining armor,
And my worst nightmare co-exist?

How am I to leave you?
When you are the music of my heart's song?
How am I supposed to stay,
When the way you hurt me is so wrong?

Swimming in love and fear,
Living with joy and pain,
Receiving your kisses and fists,
Will tonight be cuddles or blood stains?

Endless tears and confusion,
So much dread and regret,

Still hoping it's a bad dream
That's why I haven't left yet.

Black eyes filled with tears,
Sunshine replaced with rain,
My heart still deeply loves you,
While hatred fills my brain.

Remember all of the sweetness?
Of your lips so gently on mine?
I now await your fist again, Love,
For it's just a matter of time.

## Scars

Scars from the shattered glass
I walked across to get to him.
Scars from the thorns
I ran through to escape him.
Scars that have made my skin too thick,
my heart too guarded.

I've learned.
Some journeys would have been
best untraveled.
Some songs best left unsung.

But I survived, didn't I?
Despite him.
Despite me.
And I'm here now.
Risen out of the rubble.
Rebuilt.
Reengineered.
A woman revamped.

My scars make my skin thicker.
My resolve stronger.
My path wiser.
And so it is.

All of this...

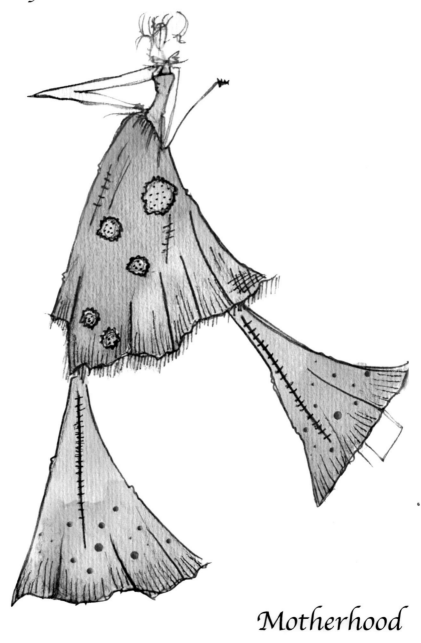

Motherhood

## My Love For You

From the very first moment
That I knew,
From that moment,
That I could feel you,
You were my truest love.

From that first sign,
Of your pure light within,
Out of that joy,
Our song began,
And so was born our love.

How could it be true?
That I could be so blessed with you?
I rejoiced in you!
Growing, glowing, shining,
And so began my love for you.

From that moment I knew, I knew,
I'd give my life, I'd go black and blue,
I'd take this whole world on, it's so very true,
There's nothing I wouldn't do for you.
And so it is my love for you.

I am only yours and you are mine.
Like a feather in the wind,
A kiss on the wings of time,
I hold my breath for your you.
I will always hold my breath for you.

I've loved you since time began,
And my love for you will never end.
Across the centuries,
Across the seas, the skies above,
And so you are my endless love.

If all else ends, if all else fails,
My little Loves, know this to be true,
There is <u>nothing</u> that compares to you,
<u>No one</u> that hails my heart as you do,

And so it is my love for you.

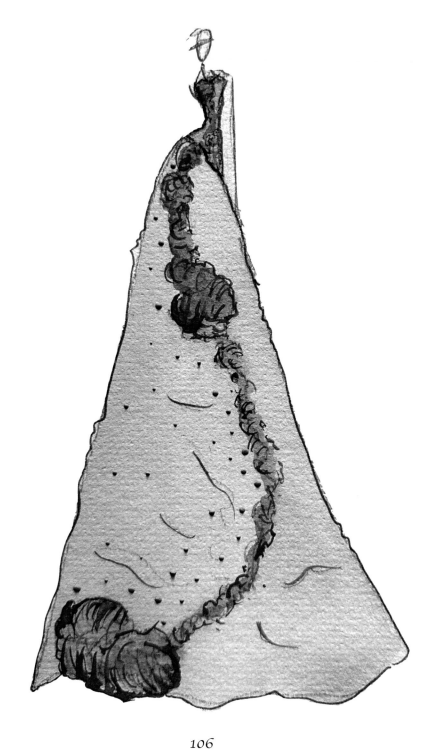

## My Little Kings

I met you on the road of Longing,
As you took me hand in hand,
My heart burst with love wide open,
And so our journey began.-

My Kings, my life is yours,
I have lived to this moment for you,
And from this very breath until my last,
I am devotedly yours in all that I do.

We splashed and played that day,
Along the water's crystal edge blue.
As the grey heron gracefully glided,
And the gentle, green lace lay softly in dew.

I looked at my First King and asked,
As his eyes sparkled crystal blue,
What will you teach me this day?
For it was what you were born to do.

At that moment, I barely caught him,
As my dancing around him led to a fall,
And although I knew he was hurting,
With tears he said nothing at all.

My heart, at the mere idea of,
Causing my Little King pain,
Like the most delicate glass it shattered,
And I vowed to never be so careless again!

"My Dear Mom, don't you understand?
A perfect you is not what I seek,
I want a mother who is brave enough,
To dance with me when I'm strong or weak!

Your love for us is without limit,
In all that we are and that we do,
Give us the gift of loving yourself the same,
Be gentle and forgiving of yourself too."

My Youngest King ran up to me now,
And the sun sparkled off his golden hair,
"My Dear King,
will you still find me beautiful?
Even when my glow and shine
are no longer there?"

"My Dear Mother, there is no beauty,
Like the beauty you are in our eyes,
As we are to you, the green in your world,
You bring the blue to our skies."

There in the forest, I began to sing,
My sons' favorite lullabies,
And suddenly the birds all joined in,
Flitting down to us from the skies.

Although my voice cracked horribly,
And I constantly changed to a worse key,
I noticed the boys smiled and hummed with me,
As if I was in perfect harmony.

As the sun glittered down through the trees,
Casting green and yellow light shows all around,
I understood for the very first time,
To them I was the perfect act, perfect sound.

My Kings, I spoke, slowing a bit,
My eyes on the earth's raw floor,
What if I just don't know the right things?
Don't know the best or need to know more?

What if I misguide the King's best ships?
Or lead his finest ponies astray?
What if you look to me for help in need,
And I fail you on your most critical day?

My tears dropped heavily onto the wide leaves,
And my heart beat hard at the thought,
Cruze slipped his small hand into one of mine,
And Neeko the other then they told what I sought:

Our, dear, sweet mother we ask nothing of you,
Except your love and acceptance, nothing more.
And just as I lifted my eyes to see them,
I heard a distant mother lion roar.

You are perfect just by being ours,
Our Queen, our Mother, our Love,
Just as we, your Sons, your Little Kings,
Are your perfect gifts from Heaven above.

Come walk through this life with us, Mom,
And let use show you the many ways,
We can share our lives and the joy they bring,
In all of our many glorious, sunny, days.

And when your gift of unconditional love, Mom,
Has turned us from Little Kings into Great Men,
We will present you with gifts to show you our love,
A new set of Little Kings for you to love again.

# The Sweet Mystic

In these novel times,
Nestled amongst giants,
Lulled into the impossible blue,
Where angels play,
I adore you.

You, with your cottontail heads,
You, with your crystal blue gazes,
You, with your child-dreams,
Your chirpings break
My long silence.

You've changed me once again.
I tumble. A pine cone at your feet.
I melt. A snowflake in your palm.
A giggle escapes me, and I cry.
For I adore you.

The songbird elevates my voice,
For there are no other words.
Moments like these on this peak,
In this deep forest,
Is an ancient dream of mine.

I pray this will be forever.
A thousand and one more
days with you,
Although I know it will not always be.

So I swim in the soaring, sweet, bliss,
Of these moments.

The earth rises to meet us.
The giants bow to greet us.
And you are mine, once again.

Within the sweet mystic,
Of this mountain.

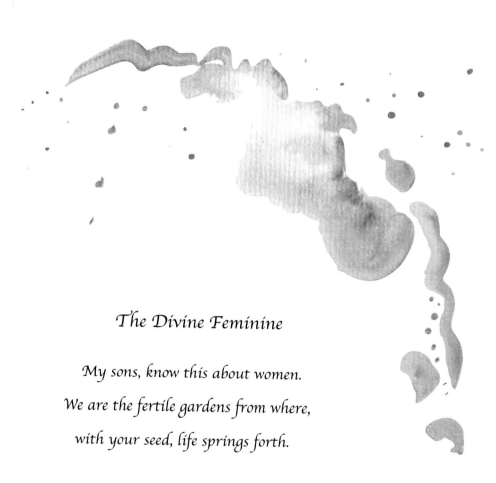

## The Divine Feminine

My sons, know this about women.
We are the fertile gardens from where,
with your seed, life springs forth.

Our arms around you provide your warmest shelter, and your strongest barrier against life's fiercest storms.

The curvy, sweet-scented softness that you love is only our outer layer.

Beneath it lies a strength so magnificent it will leave you in awe.

You will see this strength when we stand to protect our children. You will see it when we fight in the name of love.

A woman is born brave.

We aren't afraid to flood this earth with our tears and protests over injustices imposed on the innocent.

Our soft voices will soothe you on nights when you are dark and broken. These same voices will rise up and shatter the glass of injustice with such power it will shake the earth's core.

You will discover that women are wise.

If we tell you we have a gut feeling, listen closely.

For we feel vibrations that often elude you.

We grow life inside our bodies, then we bring that life into this world.

It is a physical endurance that men could not withstand.

Be in awe of women, and deeply respect us.

For after growing life in our bodies, we must then witness these very heartbeats walking independently through this life as our children.

Women do the hard day's work of men, then return home to do another full day's work as mothers and wives. It is exhausting.

Pull out our chairs, rub our feet and thank us.

Choose your woman carefully and never take her for granted.

We are emotional creatures by nature and we need your touch, your kind words and your love.

Don't assume we know.

Tell us everyday.

Know that we best relate to you when you show us tenderness and respect.

Save your grandstanding for the boys.

When you are home, show us the real you with all of your beautiful flaws.

We don't want perfection, we just want truth.

We both know that we can never match up to your physical strength. That is why you must always protect us and never lay a hand on us in anger.

Because once you break us in that way, we can never feel safe with you or protected by you again.

Our minds and bodies are complicated and we will often overwhelm you with our changing moods and thoughts.

We know you will never fully understand us, and that's okay.

We can still love each other anyway.

A woman is a mysterious, fantastical creature.

We are as unbreakable as we are pliable.

We are as strong as we are soft.

We are the cradle of life.

**We are the divine feminine.**

Choose a partner that makes you
strive to be a better man.
Treat her like a queen
and she will build you a kingdom.

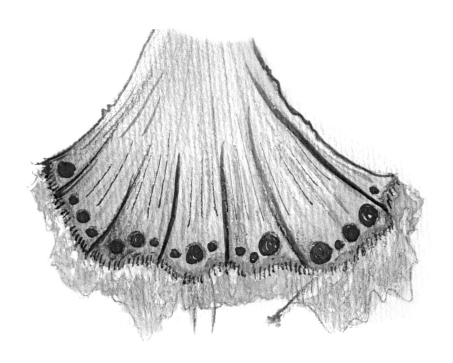

All of this...

Friendship

# A Dream

I dreamed once of my life's end,
24 hours only left to live,
What to do with such little time,
Delicate, never to have it again,
Only a day in which to give.

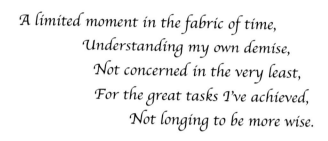

A limited moment in the fabric of time,
Understanding my own demise,
Not concerned in the very least,
For the great tasks I've achieved,
Not longing to be more wise.

Quickly I searched for those in my life,
The ones who had fluffed my soul,
Those who had been my brilliant kites,
Lifted me high, made me whole,
To thank them for being my light.

I saw my life through shiny, new lenses,
My understanding of why I was here,
The beauty overtook my senses,
My heart devoid of all fear,
Reaching out to those so very dear.

Reaching each one, I began to speak:

"You are the reason I have lived,
My life has no meaning,
Without you in my heart,
For you are the beauty in my art.

You have loved me without any limit,
You embraced me for all I could be,
You celebrated with me my life,
For each locked door you were my key,
Now in my passing, you have set me free.

Fully knowing what it means to live,
Understanding my circumstance,
I've been given the ultimate chance:
A single day to reach you now,
And thank you for this dance.

Thank you for believing in me,
When my efforts fell so short,
For your encouraging words,
Being the shade of my tree,
My strength when I needed support.

Now that my time is ending,
This is all I long to do,
Deliver to you my gratitude,
To the handful, the very few,
To the ones who loved me so true.

It's simply not about quantity,
Or the things that we make ours,
It's not about how rich we become,
Or if we've traveled to places afar,
It's about those who have loved us
for who we really are."

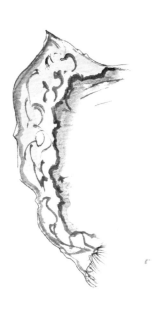

I sent this message out that morning,
Once my dream was done,
I didn't expect anything to happen,
Just another day under the sun,
Until the messages back had begun.

One after another they came,
Outpours of the most brilliant words,
Singing to me how I was cherished,
More than I'd ever heard,
My heart wrapped around every word.

My loved ones blessed me with saying,
The precious words my heart had craved,
That I had also changed their lives,
Brought smiles to them each day.
That they prayed I would always stay.

My life has changed profoundly,
From the dream I had that night.
I see things now so differently,
I no longer always need to be right.
Out of darkness I saw the light.

Each moment of life I'm granted,
Each second I'm given with you,
Is a blessing, a single thrill enchanted.
And now that I realize there are so very few,
I want to cherish each one through and through.

I hold sacred the times that you hold me,
Or simply lend me your ear,
I celebrate the very moments,
You share from your life with me,
Celebrating that you want me so near.

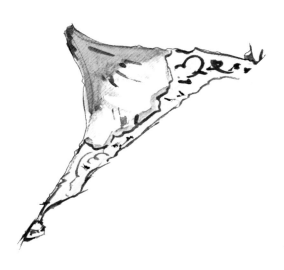

I no longer live life with drudgery,
I no longer spend time feeling low,
I now allow myself to notice,
How when you're with me,
I simply glow,
For now I understand,
I really know.

It is you, my dear ones, that have made me,
It is knowing I haven't been here alone,
Realizing just how precious each breath is,

Because the friendships with you I have sewn,
Are the greatest gifts in this life I have known.

## Wish List

This morning I'm submitting a wish list,
To her Majesty, Earth Mother, our Queen,
I've polished it to perfection,
Made sure it was sparkling and pristine.

I hope in all of her wisdom,
She will not be able to resist,
And with Her infinite power,
She will grant me what's on this list.

The first gift I request is laughter,
From small giggles to hearty guffaws,
Humor found everywhere, so often,
It defies all sensibility and laws.

And in between the laughing spells,
I quietly ask for inner peace,
An understanding so profound,
All worries desist and seize.

I also ask for patience,
And for this I can hardly wait,
The ability to not rush this life,
So all comes early, not late.

Another request, a big one,
Profound wisdom in every thought,
A keen understanding in each moment,
So no lesson is ever for naught.

And for the five great senses,
I request a thousand thrills for each,
For eyes, a fat, brilliant, orange sun,
Setting quietly over a white-sand beach.

A thousand shooting stars in tonight's sky,
To watch a soldier return home to her child,
French sunflowers with their fat faces to the sun,
A herd of mustangs running fast and wild.

To sniff, I request these heady scents,
The desert after a monsoon,
Puppy breath, a baby's sweet head,
Island jasmine in a quiet lagoon.

For the ears my request is rather grand,
Toddler laughter, barking seals, Chopin,
The rhythmic lull of a lover's heartbeat,
Hummingbird kisses and the thrill of big band.

The taste of cold lemonade from a stand in August,
Fine, European chocolates and lobster bisque,

The perfection of a deep, rich cabernet,
And the sweet sensation of a lover's kiss.

And to feel, it has to be a thousand orgasms,
Or releasing ski boot bindings after a diamond day,
The drifty, warm safety of a spoon snuggle,
Flying down a hill of fresh snow in a sleigh.

I can't forget good health and longevity,
Strength in both elbow and in mind,
Appreciation of each and every moment,
And every treasure one could possibly find.

You may think I request all of these wonders,
Because I love them all, and that is true,
But my dear friend I request these not for myself,
This wish list is what I want for you.

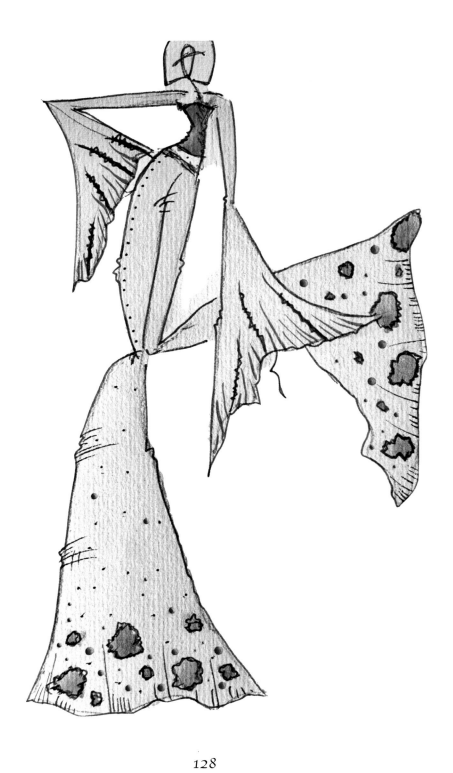

All of this...

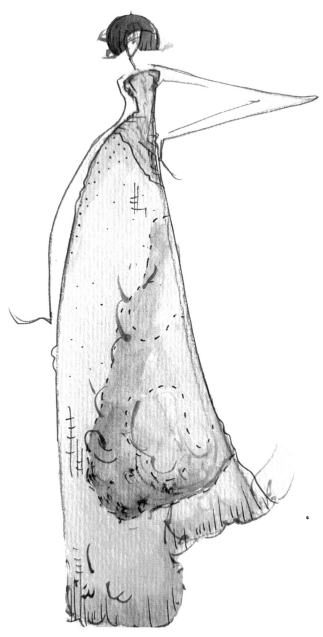

Nature

# Where The Trees Whisper

Sometimes I forget to listen,
With all of the noise of the world
drowning out the silence.
That's when she awakes me
deep in the quiet of the night,
Where the fat moon rises
And the trees whisper.
It's here that she reminds me.

It's here that she whispers her wisdom,
Reminds me that I'm so small.
Where she tells me to stop the clambering
for my imaginary finish line,
In the dark and still silence,
This is where she speaks.

"You are not really important.
Your timeline doesn't exist.
There is no finish line,
There is no race.
What matters is this moment,
What matters is that you listen.

What matters
is that you can see me,
In the baby birds,
The whispering trees,
The chipmunk chatters.
The sparkle in a child's eyes.

Stop searching for me elsewhere,
For there I don't exist.
I'm only here and now,
And if you miss this moment,
I'm gone forever.

# Forest Song

As I step among you,
I pause, look around.
Gaze up at you as I listen,
To your whispering sound.

You've been here way before
I ever existed,
And will be here
long after I'm gone.

Rising up from the ground,
Towering above me,
Arching over me
like a worried mom.

Singing your lullaby song.
Softly informing me,
"This is where you belong."

Your Majesties.
Jewels from your crowns
crunch under my weight.
As I marvel at all you create.
My air, my shelter, my calm,
And this whispering forest song.

Sing me your lullabies,
quiet and long,
Envelop me in your beauty,
tall and strong.
Whisper to me your loveliest forest song.

Our senior citizens,
Our majesties.
Our elders,
Our main stays.

Just me now,
Within the sweet silence,
Of these trees.

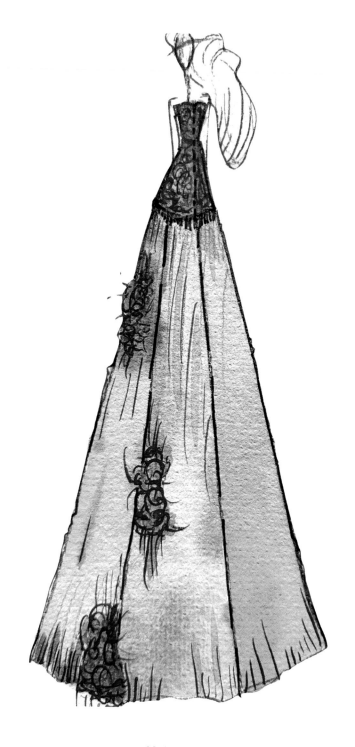

# Christmas Mountain

Sparkling, white diamonds,
Draped over a mountain's face,
Towering, green giants,
Dressed up in delicate lace.

Soft, quiet whispers,
Of the magic on its way,
The coming of a snowstorm,
Delivered on Christmas Day.

Families by their hearths,
Love and friendship abound,
Quiet crunching of wild paws,
Our forest's sweetest sound.

Blessed be this mountain,
Blessed be these trees,
Blessed be this magical place,
A snow globe filled with peace.

# Ancient Royalty

Ancient royalty draped in sparkling diamonds.

I'm rooted here.
I soar here.
I hear the earth singing.
I am reborn amidst pine cones and acorns.

Today she is decked out in her dress whites.
I escape into her kingdom.
Just my footprints now.

Rapture.
Delivery.
State of grace.

**If this isn't God, I don't know what is.**

# Good Night

And now I sleep,
Nothing more to plan,
Quiet and long,
With peace at hand.

This time is mine,
For bones and mind,
I've earned my keep,
And now I sleep.

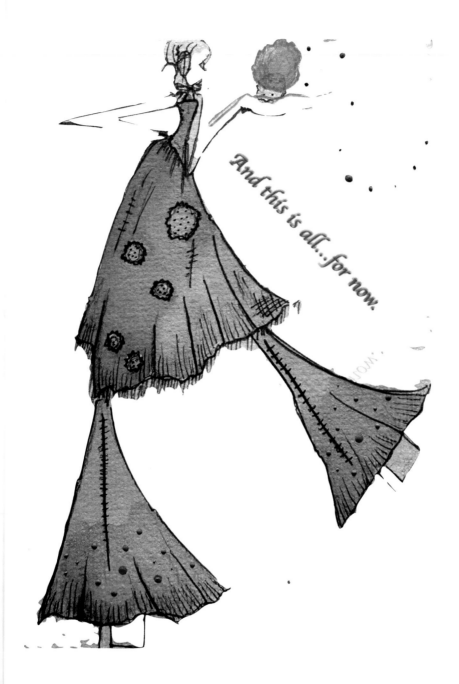

And this is all...for now.

Made in the USA
Las Vegas, NV
16 February 2024

85680903R00088